The Promise Effect

The Promise Effect

How to Create a Life That
Wasn't Going to Happen Anyway

Josselyne Herman-Saccio
& Susan Woldman Elfer

With 31 Illustrations by Susan Woldman Elfer

www.ThePromiseEffect.com

ISBN 0971586233
9780971586239

Art Direction: Betsy Woldman

Back Cover Photo: Eric Stephen Jacobs

 New York, New York

Dedications

Josselyne

In memory of my grandfather Sidney Herman who died at the age of 105 and taught me the power of PROMISING. Also to Michael whose promise to be my husband has given me the life of my dreams and the children of my dreams as well (Sophie, Sage and Shane) and finally to my parents Elaine and Harvey who are responsible for anything great in my life, their wisdom, love and generosity has empowered me to accomplish any dream I ever had, including being an author.

Susan

In memory of my father Robert and in honor of my mother Mary who have never once broken their promise to love and support me. To my husband Julian, for making it so easy to honor my promises to him. To my mother-in-law Karin Elfer, whose love and conversations have sustained me throughout the writing of this book. And to our dearest friends, Sam and Clare Minoff, whose lifetime of friendship, integrity and generosity continually inspire me. Thank you.

Acknowledgments

This book is a product of saying YES to opportunity. We would like to acknowledge the following people who have contributed to this project. A big thank you to Betsy Woldman for her art direction and brilliant eye for design. Eric Stephen Jacobs for his photography, Karen Salmansohn for her support, and Jennifer Kipley for her design layout for this book ~ and for her patience!

Contents

Contents...

Introduction

We are what we repeatedly do.
Excellence, then, is not an act, but a habit.

~Aristotle

You do not have to promise to breathe today and it will likely happen. You do not have to promise the predictable. The predictable will most likely occur. The Promise Effect uses the power of promising to help you create experience beyond the predictable, beyond the habitual, beyond the ordinary. Promising creates a life that wasn't going to happen anyway.

Why wasn't it going to happen anyway? Simple. You have to step out of who you've been in order to become someone new. Otherwise your past becomes your future therefore your future is like your past. They become interchangeable. New faces might appear in your life and new circumstances will crop up. There will be incidents of heightened emotion and times of great ease. However the content, the ingredients, will be the same in varying configurations. You will continuously move in a circle of similarity and your life will feel familiar. Why? Because it is familiar. If you see things a certain way you will continue to see things a certain way until you decide to see with new eyes. If you believe there is a limit to what you can accomplish then there will be a limit to what you can accomplish until you change your belief. If you feel you have no options then you will have no options until you make a different choice. If you do nothing new you will take your past with you by default.

Promising is a declarative action. The nature of a declaration is to bring into being something that did not exist prior to the declaration. You can promise to clean your room, change your behavior or change the world. Small or large, your promises power the engine of forward motion in your life. Born with each promise that rises in your heart is also an action plan to achieve it. If you can't figure out your next step it doesn't mean the next step doesn't exist. It simply means you are reacting out of past habits instead of responding from inspiration, drawing conclusions from what has been instead of what can be. It is when you refresh your vision and see with new eyes that opportunities come into focus and miracles occur. How do you refresh your vision? By breaking the habit of leading a predictable life. The intention of The Promise Effect is to transform habits that limit both your experience of life and the results you produce, into habits that support a life of excellence, creating the life of your dreams.

The power of The Promise Effect is in your participation with the 31 promises set forth in this book. Experts suggest that it takes an average of 30 days to break an existing habit and replace it with a new one. After thirty consecutive days you will have surpassed the threshold and your new habit, one of awakened awareness, begins with promise number thirty one, Miracle. For this reason we recommend committing to a promise a day for 31 days in numerical order. Let each day's promise build on the promise from the day before and trust yourself to integrate the benefits of each promise as you go along. In addition, you can randomly pick a promise at any time to help support you in gaining clarity in any area of your life.

The Promise Effect is an invitation. The best time to begin is now. The start of any journey is the most exciting part of the adventure because the realm of the unknown holds endless possibilities. What do you want? Or better yet, what would you want if you thought it was possible? Your promise sets the wheels in motion.

Tips

HOW TO USE THIS BOOK

1. Plan for success
Make a list of what you want to accomplish from your participation in this book. What do you plan to achieve? Clarifying your motives creates a strong foundation of support. ~ You are encouraged to get a journal to record your experiences.

2. Write out your promises
Keep your promises in existence for yourself. Write them down. Set constant reminders for yourself by placing your promise in places you will notice throughout the day.

3. Click to shift
Associate a movement with your daily promise like a click of your fingers, a clap of your hands, or snapping a rubber band on your wrist. Every time you remember your promise click your fingers (or whatever action you have chosen). This reinforces the brain connection to the new habit you are creating.

4. Set up accountability
Share your daily promise with other people so that they can hold you to account for the promises.

5. Just for today
If you feel resistant, remind yourself the commitment is to participate with this one promise just for today. Keep it simple.

6. Be gentle with yourself
If you break your promise relax. Acknowledge the broken promise and REMAKE the promise so you can keep exercising the muscle that promise is creating. Begin again.

7. Create a support group
Enlist other people to participate in THE PROMISE EFFECT so that you are not alone and you can share your experiences as you go through this book. Join our online community and post your daily progress at www.ThePromiseEffect.com

8. Acknowledge yourself
At the end of each day repeat your promise and review / record your results. Take your appreciation with you as you go to sleep.

9. Have fun
Promising creates miracles. Don't over navigate the course of events. It is when you loosen your grip that the unexpected surprises you.

~ Enjoy the miracles ~

The Promises

1

Courage

Courage

The Promise

I promise that today I will embrace a dream I hold dear to my heart and take an action towards fulfilling that dream. My commitment with this promise is to push myself out of my comfort zone and take a risk.

The Effect

Courage is not the absence of fear, but taking action with your fear. Courage responds in equal measure to the requirements you place upon it, urging you into action on behalf of the choices you make. If you are waiting for the phone to ring, an approved plan, or everything to line up, you are guaranteed a life of waiting. Refresh your dream and take a leap of faith. Once you take initiative, no matter how small or large, courage rolls up to push you through the door. Courage fuels dreams.

KEYWORDS:

adventure   power   brave   risk   initiation   dream

2

MY INTENTIONS
With all the love in my heart I put
forth my best efforts, stretching to
reach for a higher dream than I
have ever reached before, to create
a life of excellence for myself. I
intend to step into my
magnificence, in service to others
and to bring forth into
manifestation the best possible life
for myself and my loved ones, filled
with more love, laughter, joy and
success that only God could have
dreamed so big for me. Thank you!

Word

Word

The Promise

I promise to give up complaining today. My commitment with this promise is to take a moment before I communicate anything to make sure my words create possibility, honoring myself and others.

The Effect

Become aware of the creative force of language. Words are far more than descriptive tools. Words create what we see, think and feel. Isn't life exactly how you say? Every time? Aren't you, he or she, exactly how you say? Every time? Your words have infinite power. Consider you have been using that power in a limited fashion. As you express yourself with language that matches the level of experience you want to have, you become the author of the life you want to lead.

KEYWORDS:
integrity   creation   power   consequence   define   communicate

3

Attitude

Attitude

The Promise

I promise to have an attitude of joyful anticipation today. My commitment with this promise is to recognize the power I have to decide my attitude rather than settle for a default attitude that does not inspire me or the people I interact with.

The Effect

Your attitude towards any activity is reflected in the experience it holds for you. If, for example, you approach something with a negative attitude, even if your actions appear calm and loving, the outcome in the deepest sense will be negative for you. Conversely, if you have a loving attitude and find it necessary to take forceful action, the experience of love will prevail. Attitude is disposition. How you position yourself defines the direction you are moving. Where is your attitude taking you? You always have a choice.

KEYWORDS:
stance   lens   view   framework   quality   choice

Listening

Listening

The Promise

I promise to listen today without interrupting others or offering an automatic opinion. My commitment with this promise is to actually hear what people are saying versus what I'm saying about what they're saying.

The Effect

Listening requires more than ceasing to talk. Listening is standing in a space of receptivity with a willingness to learn something new. This does not mean you have to let someone talk your ear off or subject yourself to conversations that damage your well being. Use discernment. Pay attention to your inner wisdom as well. When you participate from a heightened sense of awareness, healthy boundaries are more easily established. Remember, if you listen carefully to a sea shell you can hear the ocean.

KEYWORDS:
honoring   wisdom   thoughtfulness   receptive   envelope

Power

Power

The Promise

I promise to do what I say I will do today. My commitment with this promise is honoring my word as the source of my power, exercising the muscle of saying X and doing X.

The Effect

A promise is a commitment to creating a future that would not have happened anyway. Your follow through on your commitment defines not only your character, but how the world responds to what you say. If you don't honor your word, even just a little, or think someone else should adhere, but you are the exception, then you erode the integrity of the word. From this place you cannot fully accept the truth of what others tell you, therefore missed opportunities abound. When you honor your word the world is your oyster. Why? Because you SAY so.

KEYWORDS:
empower   dignity   result   producer   strength   confidence

6

Acceptance

Acceptance

The Promise

I promise that today I will only speak positively about myself and my life. My commitment with this promise is to cherish who I am.

The Effect

Right now where you are is perfect. Your self acceptance supports your participation in self discovery. If you're holding onto beliefs about yourself that edge you out of the picture you want to be part of, let them go. Replace them with beliefs that support and uplift you. Even if it seems outrageous at first, if you embrace new beliefs about yourself you will start to see evidence of their truth in your life. You will always be a work in progress, moving forward with ease. You are lacking nothing.

KEYWORDS:
love   acknowledgement   uniqueness   satisfaction   worthiness

7

Vitality

Vitality

The Promise

I promise to participate with people and activities today with energy and aliveness. My commitment with this promise is to refresh my lust for life.

The Effect

The quality of participation in any activity is felt throughout, affecting both the process and the result. Your level of enthusiasm, whether high or low, contributes to the collective force. When you awaken your participation with a spirit of new beginnings you raise the bar of what you can accomplish. Let your inner aliveness be an inspiration. Step into your excellence!

KEYWORDS:
aliveness   well-being   energy   enthusiasm   rejuvenation

8

Balance

Balance

The Promise

I promise to identify the recurring interactions that knock me off center and, more importantly, what brings me back into balance. My commitment with this promise is to take note of the ways I naturally balance myself.

The Effect

Everything you need to live your life powerfully is within you. Situations that overwhelm you or push your buttons give you opportunity to regain your center. The more often you bring yourself back into balance the easier it becomes. Whether it's taking a deep breath, a bath, shutting your eyes, counting to ten, become aware of the things you naturally do to soothe your soul. These are your personal tools for creating balance in your life. They are always there for you.

KEYWORDS:
having-it-all space fullness harmony flexibility assimilation

9

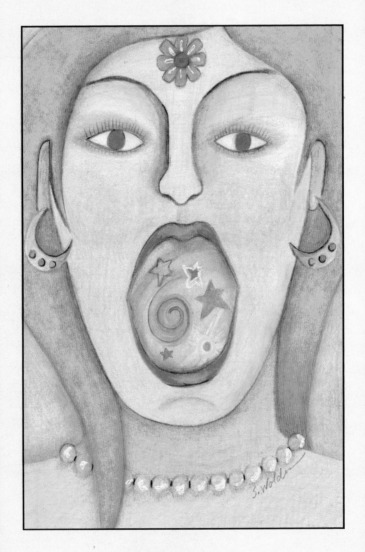

Essence

Essence

The Promise

I promise to make a list of things I want then describe how I think having each of these things will make me feel. My commitment with this promise is to get clear on why I want something so I can create it.

The Effect

You can experience having anything you desire by discovering its essence. If, for example, you want more money in your life then identify what the quality of having more money means to you. Is it freedom? Security? Happiness? If its freedom you want and you feel free when you ride your bicycle, or read a book, or sing, then do those things. Engage in activities available to you now that amplify the quality of what you want. Herein lies a secret to creation ~ You draw the form of what you want by exploring its essence.

KEYWORDS:

soul   source   oneness   core   inspiration   magnet

Game On

Game On

The Promise

I promise to play fully today, participating 100% in all areas of my life. My commitment with this promise is to completely engage with what's before me, treating each moment as if it were my only moment.

The Effect

Living a life that doesn't inspire you is the playing field of mediocrity and you are not mediocre. Can you envision the glorious mountain you want to stand on top of? Mediocrity places you halfway up the mountain. You are neither here nor there, good nor bad, impressive or invisible. If you think you are leading a mediocre life in any area of your life it simply means you are not challenging yourself to lead a better one. You have greatness to share and your soul calls upon your great self to rise up. Get in the game! Be a PLAY-A (player)!

KEYWORDS:
yes   fun   focus   participation   readiness   full-throttle

11

Having It All

Having It All

The Promise

I promise to give up excuses today that limit me in my ability to have it all. My commitment with this promise is to expand my capacity to take things on in life.

The Effect

What would your life look like to you if you had it all? What you want reflects, defines and supports who you are. The purpose of wanting something is to propel you into action towards having it. Wanting is an action point, not a destination. As you clear space in your life for what matters to you and what nurtures you, you create greater opportunity to experience those things. Gently expand your boundaries to include more. The reason you want it all is because you can have it all.

KEYWORDS:

capacity   muscle   space   worthiness   possibility   belief

12

Action

Action

The Promise

I promise that today I will empower myself by taking concrete action in respect to something I want. My commitment with this promise is to recognize that results are a product of action; no action, no results.

The Effect

Picture a wheel. The further you place yourself from the center of the wheel the more activity is required to keep the wheel moving. You're in motion, but you're not getting anywhere. It's not effective action it's a RE action and it's simply exhausting. Take a moment to get clear on what you want to accomplish and then take the action. An action sourced from your center; a space of inspiration and inner wisdom, exponentially expands the results to positively impact your life.

KEYWORDS:
just-do-it! participation effectiveness motivation inspiration

Faith

Faith

The Promise

I promise that today I will operate from a space of trust. My commitment with this promise is standing for what's possible with no visible evidence.

The Effect

Some things manifest before your eyes immediately. Other times things take form when you are not looking. Faith asks you not to depend on perceptible progress to mark the worth of a situation. It is an invitation into the state of trust where what is unlikely and impossible can and does happen. Have faith!

KEYWORDS:
vision   belief   trust   patience   surrender   higher-power

14

Happiness

Happinesss

The Promise

I promise to make a list of words that uplift me then incorporate them into all my communications today. My commitment with this promise is to consciously use language that supports my happiness.

The Effect

Happiness is a decision. Because your language creates so much of your experience, consistently using inspiring and uplifting words will positively affect you and those around you in an inspired and uplifting way. Understand this promise is like a muscle, and as you challenge yourself to shift your language sourced from happiness, your life will unfold into happily ever after.

KEYWORDS:

peace   satisfaction   sufficiency   joy   tranquility   love

Passion

Passion

The Promise

I promise to make a list of things I am most passionate about today and take an action relating to each of those passions. My commitment with this promise is to turn my inner burning for something into a tangible possibility, giving it life.

The Effect

Whether it's a natural talent, a strong interest, or something you just love to do, expressing your passion brings you into the pulse of life. This is because the underlying force of passion is something everyone shares in common. When you embrace your heart's desires others are drawn to see your worth. The value of giving life to your passion is your unique contribution to the world. Don't hold back!

KEYWORDS:
dedication   happiness   inspiration   creativity   self-expression

16

Responsibility

Responsibility

The Promise

I promise that today I will exercise my ability to re-spond to situations from a place of peace. My commit-ment with this promise is owning my part in creating my experience of life.

The Effect

You cannot choose all that happens to you, but you can choose how you respond to what happens to you. It is your response to life that creates your experience of life. When you don't see how your response contrib-utes to a situation, the situation has control over you. If something is invisible to you it has power over you. When you see it you can change it. Your ability to re-spond is your ability to choose how you respond.

KEYWORDS:
power generosity freedom creation ownership involvement

Un-Messable-With

Un-Messable-With

The Promise

I promise to be unstoppable today. My commitment with this promise is to not take things personally, therefore maintaining my connection to power.

The Effect

Standing in a space of possibility no matter what life throws at you or what people say to you is being un-messable-with. Statistics, facts and people's impressions are based on information gathered from the past. History only repeats itself if you take it with you, allowing the opinions of others to dictate what's possible for you now. Stay on track. Ground yourself in the foundation of your own experience. Remember, the most celebrated moments in history are when history re-invents itself.

KEYWORDS:
omnipotent all-of-it respect conviction self-confidence truth

18

Freedom

Freedom

The Promise

I promise that today I will explore my greatest dream as if it already exists and then take it up yet another notch. My commitment with this promise is to treat my imagination as an important tool for creating the life I want.

The Effect

You have complete freedom to think anything you choose. No matter what you are being told or what life is showing you, your imagination can take you anywhere. Loosen the grip of limiting thoughts by using your imagination to expand your inner world. At all times you are only one thought away from dreaming an even bigger dream. As you steadily bring your imagination and concentration into play, your life changes. If you can conceive it you can achieve it. This is the power of imagination.

KEYWORDS:
de-lidded   bursting   flying   exhilaration   choice   possibilities

Opportunity

Opportunity

The Promise

I promise to view life through a lens of opportunity today. My commitment with this promise is listening and looking for opportunity in every interaction and being a YES to life.

The Effect

Creating a future that wasn't going to happen in the normal course of events occurs as you hold yourself accountable for delivering on that future. That means looking for and embracing the opportunities that support you. Committing to your future self actually creates a trajectory within which all the elements necessary for this to happen start to line up. Refresh your vision and look around! Opportunities exist. It begins by saying YES to the life you want to have.

KEYWORDS:

action   attraction   expansion   progress   breakthrough

20

Perseverance

Perseverance

The Promise

I promise today to focus on something I want, but have given up on and take an action to move this forward. My commitment with this promise is to honor the process, recognizing that the journey is as valuable as the destination.

The Effect

Allow yourself to feel the elation of follow through and the steady application of self effort towards a desired goal. As you continue to do this your relationship with yourself shifts and you will start to see results. Don't give up! Within the journey itself is a wealth of experience, lessons learned, merits earned and triumph over defeat. Commit fully to what you've chosen and follow your path towards the final outcome. Your dedication pays off.

KEYWORDS:
devotion   discipline   unstoppable   focus   endurance

21

Appreciation

Appreciation

The Promise

I promise to list all the things that occur throughout my day that I appreciate. My commitment with this promise is to notice the continuous flow of blessings in my life.

The Effect

Every time you smile to yourself because of a pleasant thought, or a parking space you found, or sitting in a comfortable chair, you are in the space of appreciation. When you consciously acknowledge your appreciation you become aware of how life continuously supports you just because. Thanking someone is seizing an opportunity to not only express your gratitude, but to actually expand the portal through which blessings enter your life. The more you notice things to appreciate the more you have to appreciate.

KEYWORDS:
acknowledgement   gratitude   expansion   blessings   love

Support

Support

The Promise

I promise to support someone who needs my support today. My commitment with this promise is to recognize that supporting someone creates a partnership between us where each person is honored.

The Effect

How do you serve the company you keep? If you help someone from a position of superiority, it is both dishonoring and dis-empowering. To be in a position to support someone is a great opportunity, offering a forum to give and receive and expand your level of effectiveness. Support is a high form of respect, recognizing that all those involved, including yourself, are worthy of your time and efforts and have greatness to share. It is a beautiful and life giving exchange.

KEYWORDS:

team   community   guidance   encouragement   service

Peace

Peace

The Promise

I promise that today I will set aside a specific amount of time to sit in silence. My commitment with this promise is to give myself the opportunity to experience inner stillness.

The Effect

Quieting the mind elevates you into a higher vibration where your inner wisdom can be heard. Simply sit in a comfortable upright position and follow the rhythm of your breath. As you breathe in imagine infusing yourself with power and as you exhale imagine all the tension leaving your body. As thoughts come to you just let them be, let them float by, let them go. Calming the mind and body allows your deepest self to emerge. This creates a powerful state of being within which peace prevails.

KEYWORDS:
contentment   harmony   resolution   tranquility   meditation

24

Perspective

Perspective

The Promise

I promise to look at a situation where I've been stuck in my own point of view and approach it from another perspective. My commitment with this promise is to suspend my interpretation and see from that other perspective.

The Effect

Your view of life gives you your quality of life. As you shift your perspective in any area the quality of life in that area also shifts. Remember, just because you see something in a certain way doesn't mean it's true, it just means it's true for you. The reason it's true for you is because you choose to see it that way. Your point of view is something you have complete freedom to change. If you are willing to shift your perspective, even a little, you open to new possibilities. A shift in perspective can transform your experience of life.

KEYWORDS:
view   interpretation   filter   influence   belief   transformation

25

Forgiveness

Forgiveness

The Promise

I promise that today I will forgive someone who I have been holding a grudge against. My commitment with this promise is to experience letting go as a means to create space in my life for something new to occur.

The Effect

As long as you hold a grudge there is a piece of your heart that is shut down. Resentments have a huge price tag costing you peace of mind, connection, and living life fully. Forgiveness is giving up the right to punish someone, including yourself. To be clear, forgiveness is not a pardon. It's a release of painful emotion that has been burdening you. It is a gift you give yourself. So powerful is the shift of forgiveness that it changes you. You become someone new in the presence of acceptance.

KEYWORDS:
freedom   gift   unconstrained   awaken   lightness   peace

26

Celebration

Celebration

The Promise

I promise that today I will lighten up, laugh and have fun. My commitment with this promise is to embrace the spirit of celebration.

The Effect

The spirit of celebration takes a seat in your heart while soaring on the wings of freedom. A special event calls for celebration. The completion of a project calls for celebration. The end of the week calls for celebration. As you answer the call for celebration more often, you can experience the exuberance of celebration even as you're putting forth self effort. Celebration is not just what you do when you get to the party, it is an expression of joy.

KEYWORDS:

aliveness   joy   bliss   play   blessings   gathering   fun

27

Communication

Communication

The Promise

I promise to respond versus react to people and situations today. My commitment with this promise is to give my full attention to what's right before me.

The Effect

Don't assume others know what you want. Good communication not only requires expressing yourself clearly, but also listening with the intention to understand. When you take a few breaths before you react to someone a more authentic response will emerge that is not tangled with intense emotion. In this way you develop the ability to communicate with greater awareness, effectiveness, detachment and ease.

KEYWORDS:
listening   expressing   sharing   connecting   intimacy   honesty

28

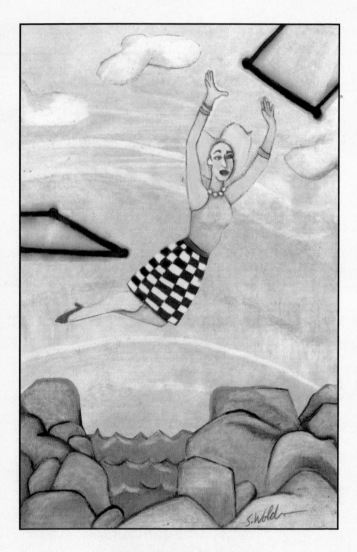

Alignment

68

Alignment

The Promise

I promise to list my values and ideals today and identify where in my life my actions are not aligned with these values and ideals. My commitment with this promise is to harness the power of integrity as a guidepost for my life.

The Effect

Your integrity reflects the values you hold dear to your heart and the ideals you wish to uphold. When you align with your integrity you are unburdened by choices which are inconsistent with your values. It is clear what to let go of and it is clear what to grab on to. This is how you move with integrity. Integrity brings clarity

KEYWORDS:
congruent   *walk-the-talk*   *ease*   *motion*   *authenticity*

29

Ripple

Ripple

The Promise

I promise that today I will be aware how even my smallest actions (or non actions) impacts my environment. My commitment with this promise is to recognize that what I say and how I behave effects my family, my community and ultimately the world.

The Effect

You are not alone, separated or isolated. As you strengthen your awareness of interconnection with everything around you, choices become more conscious and respectful towards others and the environment. If the entire universe is connected then in a very real way YOU make a difference. One small action can cause a power ripple that impacts millions. With this awareness, you become a vital part of the change you want to see.

KEYWORDS:
interdependence   legacy   contribution   responsibility   leader

30

Abundance

Abundance

The Promise

I promise to act out of a space of generosity today. My commitment with this promise is to operate as if the world is mine, the people are my guests and I am abundant enough to take care of all of it.

The Effect

Where do you feel wealthy enough to be generous? The key to leading a prosperous life is to first notice where you have already let it in. You can experience abundance through a healthy body, a sound mind, a spiritually rich life. When you shift your perception from having enough to having enough to give others you cultivate a wealthy existence. What you focus on expands.

KEYWORDS:
prosperity   fruits-of-your-labor   expansiveness   having-it-all

31

Miracle

Miracle

The Promise

I promise to stay open and available to delightful un-expected occurrences today. My commitment with this promise is to be present to life's miracles, moment to moment to moment.

The Effect

Miracles are all around you. Since miracles are not bound by the law of cause and effect, they can not be perceived by your practical mind. It is when you stop the incessant flow of continuous thoughts that some-thing miraculous happens. Your senses come truly alive. Through this lens miracles come into focus. Miracles occur naturally when you see with the eyes of love.

KEYWORDS:
unpredictable   amazing   magic   alchemy   awareness   natural

Authors' Note

It is our greatest wish that the promises in this book awaken you to the magic of PROMISING. You have begun a life changing process that gains power through repetition. For this reason we invite you to repeat the 31 promises from beginning to end or deepen your experience of a particular promise that inspired you by committing to that promise for 30 days. We encourage you to use and share THE PROMISE EF-FECT in any way that supports you in creating the life of your dreams, including inviting others to participate in THE PROMISE EFFECT.

Come join our community! THE PROMISE EFFECT community offers a wonderful message board where you can post your comments and questions and post your daily progress for accountability. If you would like to share your experiences and miracles of PROMISING please visit our website www.ThePromiseEffect.com

Josselyne Herman-Saccio

Josselyne has been working in the area of personal coaching, development, and transformative education for more than 20 years. She has led programs for Landmark Education, an international training and development company, for the past nineteen years; programs designed to inspire effectiveness and creativity in others enabling them to make their own dreams come true as well as make the world a better place.

Author of PEACE PROMISES, 30 Days to a More Peaceful Life, SO YOU WANNA BE A NEW YORK ACTOR and BEE-O-RAMA; THE A TO Z OF WAYS TO BE. She is thrilled to be working with Susan on THE PROMISE EFFECT. Josselyne is also the founder of United Global Shift, an organization dedicated to causing a united global shift in what is possible for humanity, focusing on the environment, employment, entrepreneurship, health and education. To find out more please visit www.unitedglobalshift.org

The Authors

Susan Woldman Elfer

Susan is a multi media artist, finding expression through writing, illustration, fine arts and jewelery design. A graduate of Sarah Lawrence College, Susan studied sculpture and painting in Lacoste, France and received her Master of Fine Arts degree from the School of Visual Arts in New York City where she has lived for the past twenty five years. After exhibiting her work across the United States and Europe, Susan discovered her passion for combining visual images with the written word. Her card decks and this book, THE PROMISE EFFECT, are a product of this discovery.

Susan is the author and illustrator of the CONTEMPLATION CARDS, the RELATIONSHIP CARDS, the YOGA PATH CARDS, The ASK ME! CARDS and THE BRIDE DECK. For more information on Susan's art and card decks or to order pictures from this book, please visit www.susanwoldman.com